Decision Making Made Smarter

*Clear Your Thinking, Become
More Decisive, Solve Problems
Faster, and Take Control of Your
Life*

Som Bathla

www.sombathla.com

Your Free Gift

As a token of my thanks for taking out time to read my book, I would like to offer you a free gift:

Click Below and Download your **Free Report**

Learn 5 Mental Shifts To Turbo-Charge Your Performance In Every Area Of Your Life - in Next 30 Days!

You can also grab your FREE GIFT Report through this below URL:

http://sombathla.com/mentalshifts

More Books by Som Bathla

Table of Contents

Introduction

"It is in the moments of decision that our destiny is shaped."

— Tony Robbins

Every day, we have to make some kind of decision: they add up. They could be miniature choices with minimal impact, or they could be big decisions that can change the trajectory of your life.

Simple choices may be:

- What to eat, which restaurant to visit, or what cuisine/dish to order?
- What to wear to your office or the party today?
- What route to take to the office if you are late, so you don't get into heavy traffic?

- Which movie to watch this weekend, with whom to go, and which theatre?
- Whether to go out for drinks with friends or have a fun evening with the kids?

Other times, life requires you to take a leap forward and make big decisions like:

- What career to opt for or which college/university to enter?
- Which companies to apply for jobs?
- Whether to continue in the same job, change jobs, or whether to make altogether a career move and explore new ways to reach your dreams.
- Should you marry now or wait for 3-4 years? What kind of life partner to the tie knot with?
- If you get married, do you want to have kids now or in a few years?

The above are difficult, life-altering decisions with high stakes, and the consequences will keep tormenting you for years if you don't make the right choices.

You see, all decisions are not equal, so they don't pose an equal level of challenge. Some decisions take less energy and others take lot of time, effort, and even cause a lot of stress. Any decision becomes easy or difficult depending on the stakes involved. Choosing a food item from a menu is easier than finding employment in a new sector or starting a business venture.

The bottom line is: although the nature may vary, you have to make decisions-small decisions, big decisions, every time. Every moment of your life requires you to make choices.

Therefore, it wouldn't be incorrect to say: You don't have a choice except to make a choice.

You Still Decide Even If You Think You Haven't

There's one intriguing approach a few people follow. They think if they don't make any decisions, they will remain safe from the risks involved in making decisions and the consequences that can arise. But here is the thing. Not making a decision is also a choice. Unconsciously, you may think you have not decided, but, in effect, you have chosen to ignore the situation, which in itself is a decision.

If you don't wake up after your alarm goes off and continue to stay in the bed, while you could hit the gym, you have unconsciously decided to choose laziness instead of fitness. If you are stuck in a job or are inadvertently trapped in a low-rewarding business that no longer fascinates you, and you don't do anything about it, you've made a decision to invite boredom, unhappiness and soon-to-be-highlighted issues of low performance into your life.

If you don't do anything and say you'll see what happens, then you are choosing not to improve yourself per the changing demands of the environment, thus inviting in the troubles of becoming obsolete in the marketplace. You made a decision here, although you might think you haven't.

Take this famous real-world example of what happened to a huge corporation that chose not to make a decision.

Kodak was a pioneer in film-based photography. The giant was market leader during times when cameras required inserting physical film to take pictures that later needed to be developed through a chemical process to generate a physical photograph. Unlike today's digital cameras, you had no way to know how it would look, until you saw the physically-developed prints.

Kodak continued to produce film-based cameras for decades and was ruling the industry. Despite the fact that *digital* photography was invented by a Kodak engineer, the management simply ignored the invention. During the later years of twentieth century, when digital photography was emerging, Kodak didn't pay the required attention to this new disruptive digital technology, and all but ignored the digital wave.

What was the result? New digital camera companies started enjoying dominance in the camera business, rising over Kodak, and it was not long before Kodak had to shut down its shops.

What was wrong with Kodak's approach?

Kodak just continued what it had been doing for years. It simply did not decide, and this non-decision proved to be its worst decision.

In a nutshell, you have to make decisions every time, and if you don't decide, don't kid yourself, here again you have made the decision not to make a decision.

Decision making, therefore, is the most important skill in life. If breathing is important to physical living, decision-making is the cornerstone of designing "the life of your choice".

What You'll Learn from This Book

You've made a decision to purchase this book and are already reading it shows you know the role that decision making skill plays in our lives.

My objective in writing this book is to empower your decision-making by developing the right mental framework and actionable strategies. While reading this book, you will start assessing your current situation in life, i.e., what is your level of decision making; what are the hidden barriers to effective decision making, and what are your decision making skill requirements as of now.

You'll learn the common struggles that most people face in making decision and come to know about the hidden traps that lead to bad decisions. You will know for yourself what kind of decision maker you are when you understand the four different types of decision makers and what makes them decide so different.

Like all my books, you will find this book loaded with scientific and psychological research to help you overcome your thinking bias and to equip you with new tools and parameters to decide more intelligently and make more and better decisions in less time.

Now without further ado, let's get to the next section, where you'll learn about the common decision making struggles people face.

Chapter 1: Why Do People Struggle with Decisions?

"Inability to make decisions is one of the principal reasons executives fail. Deficiency in decision-making ranks much higher than lack of specific knowledge or technical know-how."

John C. Maxwell

In my brief introduction, you already learned how decision making is all pervasive and plays a vital role in creating an optimal life. In this section, we'll start with fundamentals – let's understand what decision making really is.

What is Decision Making?

The Latin meaning of the word "decision" means "to cut off." Making a decision is about "cutting off" choices— cutting off other courses of actions and come out with a final choice among many.

Decision making is, in fact, a mental or cognitive process that results in the selection of a belief or a course of action among several alternative possibilities. It is a process of identifying and choosing the best alternative based on the values, preferences, and beliefs of the decision maker.

The definition is pretty straightforward: choosing one alternative out of many options. But the hard reality comes when we are in the process of making a decision and there are multiple parameters - the end objective, the expectations of different stakeholders, uncertainties, uncontrollable events, etc. - all of which require consideration. The complexities and factors involved in decision-making make any decision either a simple or a difficult one. The more the complexity, the harder the decision!

Some people take lot of time and still seem confused when deciding on cuisine at a restaurant or selecting an outfit.

They get overwhelmed with minute decisions, as if some hidden cloud was overpowering their entire thinking abilities. At the same time, you see people who make high-level difficult decisions without even a flinch. All the time, business leaders make big decisions like launching a new product in the market, setting up a new profitable venture despite cut-throat competition, or convincing investors to raise more funds. All these decisions require taking into account multiple parameters, a complex market environment and the needs of demanding stakeholders. You can imagine the level of decision-making skill such people have developed.

We will cover in detail the strategies and tools high-achievers have in their toolbox to make better, smarter, and faster decisions in the later chapters. But for now, let's try to understand why the majority of people struggle and the nature of their key challenges in making decisions. Here are a few factors that lead to procrastination, or making bad decisions, or not making a decision at all.

Challenges in Decision Making

Paralysis by Analysis

Paralysis by analysis is a state of over thinking and analysing a particular problem, but you still end up not making a decision; rather, you find yourself paralysed by an overdose of thinking.

One famous ancient fable of the fox and the cat explains this situation of paralysis by analysis in the simplest way.

In the story, the fox and cat discuss how many ways they have to escape their hunters. Fox boasts of having many. Cat, however, admits to having only one. When the hunters finally arrive, cat quickly climbs a tree. Fox, on the other hand, begins to analyze all the ways to escape that he knows. But unable to decide which one would be the best, he fails to act and gets caught by the dogs.

This story perfectly illustrates the analysis paralysis phenomenon: the inability to act or decide due to over-thinking about available alternatives, possible outcomes and data.

People experience that although they start with a good intention to find a solution to a problem, they often analyze indefinitely about various factors or parameters that might lead to wrong decisions. They don't feel satisfied with the available information and think they still need more data to perfect their decision. They keep on gathering more and more material, continue to interrogate more people, but, sadly, they are not able to decide anything. You'll understand the reasons more clearly in one of the later chapters about different types of decision makers and what drives their decisions.

Most often this situation of paralysis by analysis arises when somebody is afraid of making an erroneous decision that can lead to potential catastrophic consequences: it might impact their careers or their organizations' productivity, or the overall objective of the bigger team. So that's why people are generally over cautious in making decisions that involve huge stakes.

Information Overload

The next bigger challenge in decision making is information overload. People are too obsessed with collecting more and more information for making their decisions. This massive intake of information is also referred to as *infoxication* or *infobesity*. This is a situation where you collect so much information in your head that you're unable to cohesively organize and process it to arrive at any decision.

While in a paralysis by analysis situation, you keep on analysing lots of information, and due to this over-analysing, you don't find any of the alternative to be the best one, because you find fault with everyone. In the case of information overload, you tend to grapple with the sheer volume of information that overwhelms you.

Information overload occurs when the amount of input to your brain's system and cognitive faculties exceeds their processing capacity. Since you are flooded with information, you are unable to properly analyze it due to a shortage of time, resources or your cognitive bandwidth; therefore, you end up making poor quality decisions.

Clay Shirky, a professor at New York University, stated that information overload in the modern age is a consequence of a deeper problem that he calls *filter failure*. When the filters fail, we are confronted by things we have no interest in and spam starts to enter our primary inbox. In other words, you are not able to filter what is relevant and important for you, what you should consume, and how new information should come to you.

The advent of information technology has been the key driver for augmenting information overload for multiple reasons. You have enough quantity of information; there is an ease of dissemination, and the ability to spread it through outreach due to the massive output of social media, paid advertising, etc.

Psychologist George Miller of Princeton University presented one paper in psychology stating that human brain can process about seven (+/- two) chunks of information at a time. It's frequently also referred to as Miller's law. Miller says that under overload conditions, people become confused and are likely to make poorer decisions based on the information they have received as opposed to making informed ones.

We are always bombarded with loads of advertisements trying to convince us to buy things we don't need really. With too much information occupying the limited space in our heads, it becomes difficult to properly analyze a situation and make a decision.

Additional Challenges to High-level Complex Decisions

Apart from the challenges posed by excess of information, the high-stake situations pose other and different kinds of challenges, as listed below:

Uncertainty

In complex decisions, a lot of facts are unknown. If you are venturing into a new market, you don't know what factors will be impacting your launch and profitability in a given market. Every uncertainty requires us to think about and make judgements of different consequences that may arise, as well as potential probability. While uncertainty carries with it new possibilities, hasty venturing into unknown territory poses a high risk. Therefore, uncertainty makes most people stay wherever they are currently and thus end up not making any decisions.

Complexity

In high-stake decision making, there can be many interrelated factors that need to be taken in to account. Also you have to analyze the interrelationships between these factors and how each of them may be influenced by the others. When a planner develops a new city or town, there are a huge number of factors that require consideration. You have to plan, among other things, the availability of ground water, a sewerage system, building roads, and provisions for setting up an infrastructure to invite revenue-generation in the town. Just the vast number of factors makes it highly complex. Plus, the interplay among these factors makes it a strain for the brains involved to make decisions.

The Consequences have a High-Stake Impact

When you realize that the consequences of erroneous decisions are really very high stake, it immediately slows down your decision-making process. You may think it is obvious that if the stakes are so high, then decisions need to be given the more time to be analyzed before becoming final. Of course, you have to make decisions in high-stake situations, but people often get stuck and become plagued by paralysis by analysis. You will learn many effective strategies to make such decisions later in the book.

Lots of Alternatives

When you allow yourself to ponder too many alternatives, it significantly enhances the scope of the decision making activity itself. Each alternative has its set of pros and cons, and different factors and uncertainties associated with them. So comparing different alternatives, together with their associated uncertainty and consequences, creates a huge web of complexity which poses a big challenge to fast and effective decision making for many people.

Interpersonal issues

Last but not least, in the decision-making process, you need to take into account how other people are going to respond to your decisions: the reaction of all the stakeholders who will be impacted. Meeting the expectations of different stakeholders and coming up with a decision that turns out to be a win-win proposition for everyone is surely a challenge.

We covered the most common reasons that hamper the decision-making process for most people. They highlight the concern that making choices are not always a simple and straight-forward activity of selecting one out of many alternatives. It often turns out to be a stressful and demanding enterprise that requires you to put your entire cognitive machinery in full operation.

I also want to point out here that while the above challenges to decision making originate from the outside environment, there are some internal hidden traps that adversely affect your effective decision-making process and lead to bad decisions.

In the next chapter, we will talk about some major pitfalls in our thinking patterns or belief systems – the hidden traps that trip us into making bad decisions.

Let's move to the next chapter.

Chapter 2: Hidden Traps That Lead to Bad Choices

****

"Stubborn and ardent clinging to one's opinion is the best proof of stupidity."

— Michel de Montaigne

Decision making takes a lot out of us. We are nothing but a sum total of our thoughts, beliefs, and existing patterns while living our lives. Therefore, when we are confronted with making choices, it's not only those concretely visible outside factors that make the job taxing, there is also something inside of us that poses much bigger challenges.

Humans have the tendency to assign the reasons for their bad decisions to some outside factor or to the decision-making process itself. For example, the reasons may be attributed to non-clarification about the available alternatives or to a

24

lack of information to determine the cost and benefits of these different alternatives etc. But most often, the problem doesn't lie in the decision-making process; rather, it's due to something running through the mind of the decision maker.

Our thinking patterns or ingrained beliefs can sabotage the choices we make. In this section, we will talk about these mental traps, as identified by John Hammond (former professor at Harvard Business School), Ralph Keeney (professor at University of South California), and Howard Raiffa, (the author of *The Art and Science of Negotiation*), based on psychological research conducted by them over many years. These researchers stated that there are many internal hidden traps that adversely affect the decision-making process. We will now understand these major hidden traps.

Anchoring Trap

We often are influenced by the first information presented to us and give disproportionate weight to that option.

No matter what comes to us first and is later followed by a couple of other choices, unconsciously our decisions are inevitably influenced by the first set of information.

For example, how would you answer the two questions listed below?

a. Is the population of Turkey greater than 35 million?
b. What is your best estimate of the population of Turkey?

There is a huge probability that your answer to the second question will be influenced by the figure mentioned in the first. In fact, the researchers tested the above questions with a large group of people and concluded that in most cases, the instant answer to the second question was around the first figure. They also tested it by replacing the number by 100 million and, surprisingly, the answers to the second question started to come closer to the new figure.

This simple test illustrates the basic mental phenomenon known as *anchoring*. While considering any decision, our minds give disproportionate weight to the first information it receives. This first information could be in the form of initial impressions, data, or estimates that affect our subsequent thoughts and judgments.

I'm sure you must have some personal examples of anchoring experiences in your life. Assume you wanted to travel to another city or a country for the first time. As people generally do, you perform a Google search about the people in the territory. If the initial information exposed is "the people in this area are selfish", then your mind will subconsciously take note of it; and when you travel there, this first impression will remain. Your interactions and dealings with the people will be influenced by that first impression – and therefore your decisions will be colored by this anchoring trap.

Status Quo Trap

Status quo is a Latin word meaning maintaining a situation as it is. This trap biases us towards maintaining the current situation, even if better options exist. Humans generally feel comfortable maintaining the status quo, as this offers security. Take an example. Some people are highly risk averse and always put their surplus funds in low but fixed interest deposits. Now such people will continue to make the same decisions time and again despite being presented with more rewarding investment options. When posed with a new option, they might say they would think about it later, but that "later" never comes and their returns are abominable.

One experiment was conducted in which two groups of people were offered two different types of gifts of equivalent value – half of them received a mug, while the other half received a Swiss chocolate bar. They were then asked to exchange their gifts with the other group. The researchers expected around 50% of the people to happily make the exchange. But, surprisingly, the results showed that only 10% percent exchanged their gifts. That strong is the desire of people to maintain their existing situations.

People maintain the status quo because they feel comfortable and safe with the known. For them, trying something new means uncertainty, discomfort, and somewhat risky; therefore, maintaining the status quo is their natural reaction. The status quo trap affects our decision to try a newer and better option.

The Sunk Cost Trap

One of our natural tendencies is to perpetuate the mistakes of past. We tend to justify our past choices even though we see evidence that they are no longer valid. People buy real estate or some other investment and come to realization that it is a bad investment, but still they continue to hold that investment in the hope that the market will correct and eventually make up for losses. But, unfortunately, even if the market continues to tumble, they still stay invested in their original decisions.

Another example: people choose a specific career and few years later they realize that they do not want to pursue it any further. But by that time, they have already invested so much time, effort, and energy that it becomes very hard to shift their careers. I have personally gone through these phases. After spending more than one and half decade in the corporate world in the legal profession, it was a temptation to continue with that career. But somehow the drive to explore newer ways of living was stronger than continuing with my existing path, so I took a plunge to the world of entrepreneurship.

But the majority of population continues to keep justifying their past decisions and don't make new ones. Why do they behave so? Because taking a new approach means admitting that our past decisions were wrong, and frankly speaking, people are reluctant to admit to a mistake.

That's the reason a manager finds it difficult to fire an underperforming employee, because firing would indicate that the manager had made a wrong hiring decision. So the manager continues with the underperforming employees, even though that decision compounds the other errors.

In the corporate world, if an organization shows a trend of imposing severe penalties for past mistakes, then employees wouldn't change their courses of action and would rather perpetuate past decisions in the hope that the current situation will improve. Admitting mistakes could have dire consequences, so people choose to continue adhering to their past wrongs.

Confirming Evidence Trap

This trap leads one to seek out information that supports existing beliefs while discounting any opposing information.

A psychological study was conducted with two group of people: one group was in favor of the death penalty for deterring crime, while the other was against it. Both groups were provided with two detailed research papers on the effectiveness of the death penalty for deterring crime. One report established that the death penalty is effective, while the other concluded it was not.

The results of the experiment showed that despite being aware of detailed scientific research on arguments and counter-arguments regarding the death penalties, each group became more convinced about the validity of their own position. People simply accept information that supports their pre-conceived notions and dismiss the conflicting information.

Why does this happen?

It is our tendency to subconsciously decide what we want to do before we even figure out why we want to do. We are also naturally inclined to engage ourselves in the things we like rather than in things we don't like. Thus, we tend to find arguments for what we like and simply reject information that doesn't support our likings. Chip Heath, author of the book *Decisive,* rightly states:

> *"When people have the opportunity to collect information from the world, they are more*

likely to select information that supports their pre-existing attitudes, beliefs, and actions."

Framing Trap

This trap plagues us when we make the mistake of framing a problem or question appropriately. The way a problem is defined can significantly influence one's choices.

The same problem can elicit very different responses when framed using a different reference point. Let's assume you have $2,000 in your bank account and are asked the following questions:

- Would you accept a fifty-fifty chance of either losing $300 or winning $500?
- Would you accept the chance?

What if you were asked this question?

- Would you prefer to keep your checking account balance of

$2,000 or accept a fifty-fifty chance of having either $1,700 or $2,500 in your account?

You can see that the two questions pose the same problem. While your answers to both questions should, rationally speaking, be the same, studies have shown that many people refuse the fifty-fifty chance in the first question but accept it in the second. Their different reactions result from the different reference points presented.

The way a question is framed has an immediate impact on the way you will make decisions.

Recallability Trap

This trap gives undue weight to recent and dramatic events. As human, we tend to give more importance to recent memories and events with the most effect. We frequently base our predictions of future events based on past memories and events that are either recent or have some dramatic element attached to them.

For example, say you have to decide and finalize your next vacation location, and you have several options in your mind. But suddenly you remember that you recently heard about a heinous rape and murder incident that appeared on the news channels. Now even if that country has high security measures and zero-tolerance policies regarding tourist safety and protection, your first inclination is to base decisions on the recent dramatic event instilled in your memory, prompting you to rule out going on vacation to this country.

Lawyers often get into the recallability trap when defending a liability suit for clients. This is because the huge awards are highly publicized in the news and social media everywhere, while a large number of suits get lost in the shuffle. This recallability trap prompts courts to offer huge settlement amounts, more than is actually needed.

All of these hidden traps unknowingly come in the way of making decisions. If one is not aware of internal self-nurtured biases over a long period of time, they will lead us to making bad decisions. But once you are aware about them, you become more objective in your assessments and a take different perspective before arriving at any decision.

We talked about the challenges to decision making and the hidden internal traps that lead to bad decision. However, in addition to this, every decision maker has certain pre-set expectations that come along with a particular decision, which in turn affect the way they make future decisions. In the next chapter, we will talk about different types of decision makers; you can identify what kind of decision maker you are.

Chapter 3: 4 Types of Decision Makers: Who Are You?

****

"Decision is the spark that ignites action. Until a decision is made, nothing happens. Decisions are the courageous facing of issues, knowing that if they are not faced, problems will remain forever unanswered."

~Wilferd Peterson

We all see, few people seem to make decisions fast compared to those who take ages to make even a regular decision. Why is it so?

Why do these people have different aptitudes to decision making? What is the key factor that drives their decisions?

There is one more important element that affects decision making efficiency –

and that is the end objective to be achieved out of that decision.

Barry Schwartz, an American psychologist and author of *The Paradox of Choice,* states that one of the most important elements that governs the decision making approach of different people is the end objective.

Behind every decision of a decision maker, there is some purpose or objective. Depending upon the end objective desired from any particular decision, there can be four categories of decision makers. Let's understand each of these; then you may ask what you think about yourself.

Maximizer

The Maximizer is the person whose end objective is always to look out and opt for the best alternative. Therefore, first he takes enough time to find as many alternatives as possible before making a decision. Although this type of people know they have made the best choice after thorough analysis, still if they come across something better, they again start to think about getting the next best solution. They always want to maximize the benefit.

Let's understand this type with the help of an example. For example, you have already purchased a pretty decent outfit to attend a party in town from one of the best shops. But as you purchased it and moved to the next store, you see a different outfit – much better than what you just bought. As you have found the next best alternative now, you start feeling bad about your previous decision despite the fact that that the previous alternative met your requirements, until you saw the new one.

This is an example of the Maximizer – who tasks himself with making the most informed and intelligent decisions after exploring the best possible alternatives.

If you seek and accept only the best, you are a Maximizer. Maximizers need assurance that every purchase or decision they make is the best possible.

Satisficer

The next type of decision maker is the Satisficer. The concept of "satisficing" was proposed by U.S. Nobel Prize winning economist, Herbert A. Simon, by combining the two words "satisfying" and "sufficing".

Satisficers are people with a specific criteria or parameters to be fulfilled for making decisions. Of course, they choose their parameters, which requires exploring the best available alternatives, but unlike Maximizers, they set a standard, which if met, they will make the decision. Once Satisficers get a thing or make a decision based on their own set of standards, they are happy with that decision; and if some next best alternative pops up, they will not get dissatisfied, unlike the Maximizers.

For example, if you want to buy a car and you have certain important standards you want to see in the car, now you'll start exploring and compiling various available alternatives. Suppose you have a preference for safety and space in the vehicle as compared to design. Once you find a vehicle that addresses your standards of safety and space, you make your decision to buy that particular vehicle and don't bother about other options that might come up, which might be better than your previous decision – because your choice meets your given standards.

Therefore, a Satisficer settles for something that is good enough and doesn't worry about the possibility that something better may come up later. To put it simply, a Satisficer keeps on finding an alternative based on his or her set of standards; and the moment it is found, they stop searching further.

That doesn't mean that Satisficers settle for low standards; their criteria can be very high; but as soon as they find the right alternatives be it a house, car, or food with the qualities they want, they're satisfied.

Perfectionist

Let's now look at this third category of decision makers - the Perfectionist. These are the people who keep on exploring their options until they find the perfect one. They think that their decisions need to be flawless, which no one will question, and, therefore, until they reach this level, they keep on exploring the alternatives.

The Perfectionist likes to achieve the best, like the Maximizer. But there is a key difference. While both have a high standard of performance they want to achieve, Perfectionists have very high standards that *they don't expect to meet*. By contrast, Maximizers have very high standards and *they expect to meet* them.

Therefore, it happens that Perfectionists may not be as happy with the results of their actions as Satisficers, while they seem to be happier with the results of their actions compared to Maximizers.

John wooden, an American basketball coach, once said that perfection is what you're striving for, but *perfection is impossibility*. However, *striving for perfection is not impossibility.* Therefore, he advised to do the best you can under the conditions that exist: that is what counts.

Optimalist

Now comes the last category of decision makers — Optimalists. An Optimalist is someone who is mindful of and deals with the constraints of reality. They know that nothing will ever be perfect, so they are kind of *ambitious Satisficers.*

In a sense, the Optimalist is not satisfied with good enough; they are ambitious; they want more. On the other hand, they are not *maniac Maximizers.* They are somewhat in between of Maximizers and Satisficers.

To summarize, a Maximizer will never be happy, because the moment he sees something better than what he has chosen, he will start regretting his past decisions. No matter how good something is, if a Maximizer discovers something better, he will always regret having failed to choose it in the first place. Maximizers are prone to experience a sense of "buyer's remorse" following any purchase decision.

To avoid the kind of regret the Maximizer faces, perfection is comparatively a better approach, because Perfectionists know they have standards they don't expect to meet. But, unfortunately, perfection is not achievable – the journey to perfection is endless, exhaustive, and paralysing in the constant consideration of multiple alternatives. So the Perfectionist is not happy with their decisions, but they are still better than Maximizers. You can't achieve perfection; you can only strive for perfection and thus keep on improving.

But as compared to Maximizers and Perfectionists, Satisficers' stakes are not that high. Therefore, the possibility of regret in the case of the Satisficer is much less, almost negligible; for them perfection is unnecessary.

The last category of Optimalist is something everyone should strive to achieve because an Optimalist is really considerate of the hard core realities of what is achievable and what is not, what is controllable and what is not. He knows that things can't be perfect, so he chooses to strive for perfection; but he won't face regret like Maximizers.

I hope the above categorization of decision makers will give you enough reference points to analyze your own behaviors and actions, and to find out which category you fall in. As for any treatment, you must first make the right diagnosis before accepting a prescription. You should check your own patterns and analyze what end objectives you want to meet when facing a decision problem. This distinction between the four categories of decision makers will help you fine-tune your approach and thus improve the quality and pace of your decision making.

With that, let's now move on to the next chapter.

Chapter 4: Overcome Your Biased Thinking

****

"The confidence people have in their beliefs is not a measure of the quality of evidence but of the coherence of the story the mind has managed to construct."

~ Daniel Kahneman

Though we may think this way, making a decision is not merely the rational and logical process of simply choosing between one out of a few options. Most often you make decisions that have nothing to do with logic; rather, they are carried out based on your own prejudices or certain biases about the situation, circumstances, or people around you.

One such prevalent bias is confirmation bias, which can also be considered as the mother of all biases, and most people suffer from this prejudice. Under this bias, whenever you are presented with some new idea or thought, you simply try to find evidence that confirms your previous beliefs and negate all other information. The point is that the confirmation bias plagues your thinking in a way that forms a myopic view; you look only for evidence that supports your preexisting beliefs.

One of the world's best-known sceptics and critical thinkers, Michael Shermer, author of *The Believing Brain,* has explored the reasoning of people who are so stuck in their beliefs. He puts it bluntly:

"We form our beliefs for a variety of subjective, personal, emotional, and psychological reasons in the context of environments created by family, friends, colleagues, culture, and society at large; after forming our beliefs we then defend, justify, and rationalize them with a host of intellectual reasons, cogent arguments, and rational explanations. Beliefs come first, explanations for beliefs follow."

I have covered many such biases that stick like a bug in your mind and how you can debug it in my other book, _Mind Hacking Secrets_, where you learn about all the cognitive biases in much greater detail.

Now in this section, we will talk about some further mental biases or false assumptions that inhibit the objective decision-making process. I will briefly explain the bias and then we will talk about ways to conquer it.

Use Observers Perspective

Often, the way we make decisions for others is not the same as would make for ourselves. We give advice to others that we personally wouldn't implement so easily. For example, if your friend, who just took a new job, seeks advice about how to approach her manager and explain her inability to fully understand some office-related project. Most probably, you would do the following.

You would check with her whether she had tried other ways to resolve the issues on her own. Assuming she answered in the affirmative, your quick advice to her would be to directly approach the manager and seek clarification about the project.

That seems like a pretty obvious advice, doesn't it?

However, assume you had a similar work-related problem. Would you still do the same thing? Probably you would not be that quick in approaching your manager, unless you had a very friendly relationship with him or her. You might hesitate due to the fear of being rejected. You might fear being considered naïve or get anxious thinking that your boss might mistake your lack of knowledge as incompetency.

The reality is: when you personally experience some problem and want to make a decision about it, your decisions are influenced by your emotions. But you don't come across such emotions when you advise others in choosing similar decisions. This is because while advising your best friend, you would tend to objectively examine the situation and offer an independent opinion. You don't feel the emotions your friend experienced in a particular situation and therefore your advice now is to a large extent objective and rational.

Here is the best piece of guidance we can give when you are getting indecisive about any situation -- take an observer's approach. Try to think about how you would look at the situation as an independent person? Try to imagine what you would advise your best friend in such a scenario.

The observer approach will help you form an unbiased and unprejudiced view about the situation, and you can make your decisions faster this way. Such an approach gives you solutions from an objective perspective, as if advice from an outside person related to your problem.

Beware of Liking or Mirroring bias

Have you ever had the experience where a buying decisions became influenced merely by the sales person telling something good about you or related to you?

Sales persons often use these tactics. Try to remember some instance when you were out there buying an outfit for a wedding in your family and a sales clerk told you, "This dress suits you well", or maybe "you've made a very good choice". Maybe you wouldn't realize it at that time, but flattery generally has a great impact and there are good chances that similar behavior influenced your decision to buy from that sales person.

This influence on behavior is called "liking bias". We generally fall prey to this bias – i.e., liking people similar to us and who like us. *The psychology in the field of sales shows that people tend to buy only from people they like.*

If you have a choice of buying groceries or cosmetics from two shops, you'll unconsciously choose to go to a store you like or where you feel comfortable with the manager or representatives. If you think that the store manager of a particular store is polite, respectful, and cheerful, you'll be more inclined to buy from that store. That's why in sales training, the sales persons are explained the importance of behaving well and maintaining a level of connection with customers, so they can sell better and more to those customers.

Another technique sales people use is "*mirroring*," or copying the gestures, facial expressions and language of the client. For example, if your manner of expression is through hands movements or using a specific kind of language, and the person in front of you uses the same gesture or similar language, you immediately start to feel a connection or instant rapport with that person.

I personally experienced this a number of times during a short stint in a corporate job in Mumbai, the western part of India. I didn't know the local language (Marathi). I noticed that most of the time while interacting with government officials like the police or any other officers, if someone spoke in the local language, the officers felt immediately connected (as if they were family members) and appeared much more forthcoming to help. My office colleagues would talk to them about official work only in the local language, which helped them to instantly build rapport. It was a clear evidence of "mirroring" in action.

Mirroring helps salespeople appear similar to clients, thus more likeable and more likely to close the deal.

Hence, don't let others affect your decisions to your disadvantage through the ploy of mirroring. Merely knowing the psychological biases of "liking" and "mirroring", you'll realize that your decisions start improving while making you decisions.

However, you should try these biases to influence others when selling your ideas or thoughts, if you want to get along with people and make progress.

Be Mindful of Unconscious Associations

How they influence your actions?

Unconscious associations **influence our actions** in a very specific way. If you unconsciously associate yourself or think of yourself like someone, your decisions and actions will change accordingly.

These unconscious associations tend to form over a period of time when staying in a similar environment for a long time. Your environment makes you think or believe about yourself in a particular way – forming a self-imposed identity. There is a famous saying: *"Identity precedes activity."*

There was a 1998 study[1] conducted on a group of people. The subjects were asked to play Trivial Pursuit (a board game popular in Canada and the US) to test general knowledge. But the experiment involved one specific element. Before starting the game, the participants were divided into two groups and asked to perform an imagination exercise. The first group was asked to imagine themselves as professors and think like professors. The second group was asked to imagine themselves and think like they were soccer hooligans.

The result showed that the performance of the two groups differed. The group that thought like an "intelligent"

[1]

https://www.ncbi.nlm.nih.gov/pubmed/9569649

professor got more right answers than the group that thought like "dumb" football hooligans. Regardless of their level of general knowledge before the game, their association with a specific identity significantly influenced their performance.

Malcolm Gladwell in his book, *Blink,* notes: "*[Experiments] suggest that what we think of as free will is largely an illusion: much of the time, we are simply operating on automatic pilot, and the way we think and act – and how well we think and act on the spur of the moment – are a lot more susceptible to outside influences than we realize.*"

The key takeaway here is to disengage yourself from negative mental associations and, rather, form some powerful positive associations. If you don't know some skill, don't connect negative association of yourself with the image of a poor performer. Rather, you can opt for online classes or start speaking to mentors and generate a positive association of yourself as a person with a growth mindset who is a keen learner. This simple approach of looking yourself differently will definitely help you change your actions accordingly.

How do they influence your behavior?

These unconscious associations not only can change our course of action, but they also have the power to **influence our behavior**.

Take an example: most of the population has learned to unconsciously and automatically associate attributes like "white," "male" and "tall" with qualities like power and competence. Although we may not explicitly admit that tall, white men are more competent than short, black women, many of us form these associations unconsciously.

There was a study that showed that it is easier to be professionally successful as a tall, white male. A 2004 study by psychologist, Timothy A. Judge, Ph.D., of the University of Florida, and researcher, Daniel M. Cable, Ph.D., of the University of North Carolina, found that *a one inch increase in height turns into a measurably higher salary*, and top management positions are almost exclusively held by white males of above-average height.

One classic example of such an unconscious association is Warren Harding, former US president. He is evidence of how associating general external characteristics with certain skills can turn out to be a blunder. Harding was elected President of the United States after the end of World War I because his supporters simply thought he looked like a president - because he was a tall, white man. But, apparently, he had no real skills or merits; and as often reported[2], he was widely considered one of the worst presidents of all time. People elected him based on the unconscious association or assumption that white, tall men possess the characteristics or traits that make for a high profile position.

Unfortunately, unless we are self-aware of these limitations, they strongly

---

2

http://content.time.com/time/specials/packages/article/0,28804,1879648_1879646_1879696,00.html influence our actions and behaviour unknowingly. Therefore, you need to objectively test your/specific assumptions on pre-determined parameters, rather than being misguided by your unconscious associations.

Learn How to Shift Autopilot behavior to Manual Behavior

Most often, due to behaving in a particular way for a long period, we start to behave in that way, almost on an autopilot basis.

When we make certain types of actions day after day on a mechanical basis only, we don't notice the gradual changes that, over time, can lead us to a drastic situation.

To avoid this mental trap, we need a figurative "tripwire": a signal that makes us aware of our autopilot behavior, and, if necessary, prompts us to correct it. One way to do that is to establish clear signals to interrupt any "autopilot behaviour", because by repeating that behaviour an infinite number of times, you become so numb that minor nudges don't work anymore. So, you need some kind of tripwire arrangement that will provoke a kind of shock that immediately disturbs your autopilot thinking pattern.

Let's take one example of a tripwire the American shoe seller, Zappos, follows systematically. Zappos has a program[3] that pays new employees $4000 to quit the company during the initial training sessions. The policy is designed to make sure that new employees are committed to working at the online retailer beyond just a pay check. This move ensures that once new employees feel they don't like working there anymore, they're encouraged to take the money and leave.

This is a tripwire to help staff see their situation clearly. It interrupts indecisive behavior of otherwise unmotivated employees based on habit and prompts conscious decision-making. This is a win-win proposition because on the one hand, it helps unmotivated staff make a

[3] https://www.inc.com/david-burkus/why-amazon-bought-into-zappos-pay-to-quit-policy.html

decision, and on the other hand, it helps Zappos get rid of underperforming personnel.

Offer Deadlines or Partitions

One method to change autopilot behaviour is to create deadlines to keep yourself from falling into bad habits. Deadlines help us enforce a decision we'd otherwise procrastinate on.

One of the six elements of influence, as propounded by Robert Cialdini in his great book, *Influence,* is the element of scarcity or urgency. As humans, we even don't take the best action for us when there is no urgency - sadly that's how humans behave. We keep on delaying even if we know that a decision is best for us, thinking we will do it someday later. But as soon as we realize that we will miss out on the chance to avail some offer, we immediately take action. Deadlines trigger the autopilot behaviour of not taking action.

Along these lines, another study was conducted where the researchers offered college students $5 to fill out a survey.

Initially they were not given a timeframe. Despite the fact that they would receive money to fill out the survey, the students were not forthcoming. Later, when given a five-day deadline to complete the survey, 66% of the students collected the money; but without a deadline, only 25% collected it.

Another effective approach to trigger behavior is *to make partitions*, meaning dividing the reward in various parts to keep incentivizing the action. For instance, if you look at the venture capital investment world, instead of handing out one huge sum to the entrepreneurs, large investments are distributed by dispensing smaller sums over time. This is done to prompt the conscious attention of the entrepreneur, serving as a tripwire that doesn't let people to get into a comfort zone and slack off. Therefore, each round of partial investment serves as a tripwire to make sure that everything is going the right way.

Let's talk about one final method that works to get people out of their autopilot behavior. It is by way of *using labels* to recognize disturbing (or encouraging) patterns. For example, in their training, pilots are introduced to the concept of *leemers*, which describes *"the vague feeling that something isn't right, even if it's not clear why."* Having a name for this feeling means that pilots are less likely to ignore their feelings. Once a name is given to the feeling, its existence is acknowledged. It becomes important because when they are responsible for the lives of so many people, such that even a nagging feeling can act as a tripwire prompting them to pay conscious attention to the situation.

Being aware of your internal biases and using strategies to overcome them will help you make better and more effective decisions. Even knowing these biases exist will make you stand on a platform above other people who are unaware of them.

Now let's move on to the next chapter, where we will learn how much information we should look for in order to make effective decisions.

Chapter 5: Do You Really Need More Information?

"The key to good decision making is not knowledge. It is understanding. We are swimming in the former. We are desperately lacking in the latter."

— Malcolm Gladwell

A proper decision requires an optimal amount of information. Too much information and you'll be stuck analysing and eventually fail to make a choice. On the other hand, too little information, and you'll be stressed and anxious about your decision going wrong.

Hence the important questions are: how much information do you really need before making a decision? Also, what kind of information must you consider as necessary and what information to simply ignore?

Let's learn about some of the best techniques to optimize your approach to gathering the most relevant information.

Don't always decide in Yes or No

You don't have to always make decisions in the form of yes or no. Take an example: if your friend asks you to accompany her to a movie this Friday, you may find it difficult to answer directly in yes or no. Saying yes to this option might require you to reschedule other pre-commitments, while on the other hand, refusing your friend will make you feel like you are sacrificing your desire for entertainment, and maybe your friend won't be very happy with you if you simply reject her option.

Then what do you do?

You should think about whether there are other alternatives during the time your friend has proposed a movie. Maybe you have the option of celebrating an evening out with family over a dinner, or you could have a get together with a few old friends to share experiences. You might ask your friend to go to a book fair or an exhibition, which you think is a better and more enriching experience. Remember, you'll always have many choices instead of limiting yourself to simple option of yes or no.

One study conducted at Southwestern University, Texas involved 150 students. The results demonstrated that when student participants were given a choice between buying a video they liked for $14.99 or not buying it at all, only 25% didn't buy it. But when the wording of the negative choice also stated, *"Keep the $14.99 for other   purchases,"* 45% didn't buy the video at all.

Since the choice itself remained the same in both cases, this example shows that just a subtle suggestion about the existence of another alternative is enough to improve decision-making. In terms of economics, this concept is known as "opportunity cost" – meaning what other opportunities you would lose by exercising the present option.

Therefore, if the decision to be made is posed in the terms of "take it or leave it", you'll be forced to choose it or reject it...But if you are slightly nudged to other alternatives, it will expand your thinking horizon, and now you will consider these other alternatives as well.

Don't forget – your best decisions will always come from your best alternatives.

Multi-tracking of Information

We often try to solve a problem by implementing the one option that seems best. However, trying out just a few more options simultaneously can yield much better results. This approach of trying multiple options together is known as multi-tracking, and it has the potential to improve one's cognitive abilities and thus the decision-making process significantly.

In one research experiment, two groups of graphic designers were given an assignment of making a banner advertisement for an online magazine. The first group created just one advertisement at a time, receiving feedback after each round. The second group, however, began their process with three ads, which received direct feedback, and then they narrowed the choice down to two options. On the basis of the next feedback round, they arrived at a definitive result.

The ads of the second group were rated higher by magazine editors, independent ad executives, and in real-world tests.

Why was it so?

It was because by simultaneously working on several ideas, the designers in the second group were in an advantageous situation, as they were able to directly compare the feedback on each of the design during each round of work, and thus, they could incorporate the client's suggestions on three different designs constructively into one single ad design.

Multi-tracking not only can result in higher-quality work, but as studies have shown, exploring several alternatives at the same time actually speeds up the decision-making process.

Another reason this works is because by having more alternatives, you're less invested in any single option, which allows you to remain flexible with either of the options, whereas if you work on only one design, you'll be highly invested in success of that design, adversely affecting your flexibility.

I closely relate the above study with my personal experience while engaging designers for my book covers. I have one designer, who always reverts with two different sets for each book cover. It helps me see two different alternatives at one go. With this level of flexibility, I can either select one out of two options or else I can pick the best elements of both designs and the let the designer know my feedback to make further changes. Here the designer is more flexible with either of the options to make needed revisions.

To make your decision-making process more effective, try to adopt a few different approaches together.

This approach reminds me about the principle of "Take massive action", as Tony Robbins, world-renowned strategy coach suggests. How? This is because working on multiple tracks for one project requires you to put in additional time and effort simultaneously to deliver different options. Here is the benefit – by working on different options, you put more thinking and effort into the project. You start to see the different ways your project can come out. Finally, massive action shows your mistakes, if any, in the early stages and, therefore, you can correct your course of action, which enriches your experience and makes you wiser about making better future decisions.

But, there is a caution – you need to avoid the "choice overload" problem, as we'll discuss in the next point.

Avoid Choice Overload

We often say "the more the merrier", but, unfortunately, it's not true in many cases, including in making choices – paying attention to too many choices is a guaranteed roadmap to indecision.

Companies often assume that if they offer their customers more choices, they'll be more likely to buy the products since they'll find what they are looking for. This way, we think our customer will find *exactly* what he or she likes.

But here's the paradox of choice: if a person is presented with too many choices, he or she is actually *less likely* to buy.

In 2000, psychologists, Sheena Iyengar and Mark Lepper, from Columbia and Stanford University published research about jams[4]. The research was conducted inside an upmarket grocery store, where the researchers put a tasting booth for the store customers to taste different kind of jams and choose the best. On one Saturday at rush hour in the grocery store, 24 varieties were presented. However a week later on Saturday for the same time duration, only six different varieties of jams were presented before the consumers.

The results of the study were surprising. It showed that on the 2nd day, by showing only 6 types of jams, the organisers were able to sell ten times

----

[4]
https://faculty.washington.edu/jdb/345/345%20Artic les/Iyengar%20%26%20Lepper%20%282000%29.pdf

more, as compared to the first day. The researchers concluded that while the big display table (with 24 jams) generated more interest, people were far less likely to purchase a jar of jam than in the case of the smaller display.

Why was it so?

It was because the customers were overwhelmed with the number of choices presented before them, and they couldn't decide which one they liked the most. In such a situation, the ultimate reaction is not to decide anything - so they didn't buy. While too more choices seems to be appealing at the first sight, choice overload paralyses the customer.

Therefore, while the previous illustration of multi-tracking is definitely a better idea as compared to pursuing just one plan action; it can be seen, however, that if someone is bombarded with too many choices, overwhelm and indecision will be the only consequences.

Avoid All Irrelevant Information

The immediate attention span of human beings has been drastically reduced, thanks to the advent of technologies and most particularly smart phones loaded with unlimited internet access. A recent study[5] was conducted by Microsoft Corporation, showing that the human immediate attention span has declined to *eight* seconds only. To give you a comparison, a goldfish (notorious for the worst attention span) has an immediate attention span of *nine* seconds.

To make better decisions, you need to focus your attention on the aspects that really matter. You need to avoid or get rid of any information or things that don't contribute positively to your most important decisions. In effect, you need to cut out all the irrelevant information.

That's why Apple's Steve Job's closet was filled with dozens of identical black turtlenecks and Levi's 501 jeans - to simplify his choices. That's why a former US President once said, "'You'll see, I wear only gray or blue suits. I don't want to make decisions about what I'm eating

---

[5] https://www.medicaldaily.com/human-attention-span-shortens-8-seconds-due-digital-technology-3-ways-stay-focused-333474

or wearing because I have too many other decisions to make.'

Why do all these high-achievers cut short on all the routine decisions? Because they know the concept of "decision fatigue" Psychologists explain that our minds have a limited amount of willpower. The more decisions we make, the more willpower is consumed. Therefore, it's better to safeguard our willpower for only those decisions that are most important for us.

A strategy called *"Elimination by Aspects Model"* was proposed by Amos Tverskey, a cognitive psychologist. In this approach, you evaluate each of the available alternatives by measuring them with one parameter at a time, beginning with the most important for making the decision. When a particular alternative doesn't meet the parameter you have established for your end objective, you instantly delete the item from your list of options. Your list of possible choices gets smaller and smaller, as you eliminate items until you eventually arrive at just one alternative.

I was not aware of this technique until recently, but, unknowingly, I have been using this technique for most of my life - from the simplest to the most complex decisions. For example, the technique I used in making a big decision was to shift my family to a new city to take up a new challenging job. I gave more weight to my personal growth and didn't give much to the comfort level I could have maintained by staying in my town. While deciding, I eliminated those elements that were less significant and finally closed on the one that was more important to me. Also, I have been using the technique more recently in helping my spouse shop for clothes. I simply start by eliminating dresses one by one based on how they look on her.

This process of elimination by aspects is a great strategy to cut your choices down only to an important few, so you don't get paralysed by choice overload.

Follow the 40:70 Rule

There are times when you have to make decisions in the face of a high degree of uncertainty. You realize that there is not enough data or information upon which you can base your decisions. A lack of complete information puts you in state of anxiety, and you don't move any further along.

Here you can use Colin Powell's 40-70 rule when you are not sure about the adequacy of available information. Former U.S. Secretary of State Colin Powell devised this rule about making decisions to show how one arrives at a point of action when you lack sufficient information.

He suggested that whenever you want to make some decision on an important project, which involves uncertainties about future outcomes, you should have no less than 40% and you don't need more than 70% of the information to make a decision. He states that less than 40% of information means we are bound to make wrong decisions. If we continue to search for more than 70% information, we will end up taking so much time that the decision itself will not deliver meaningful results, because it's already too late.

This rule is not some blind hasty suggestion. While it doesn't rely on securing 100% information, it still recommends having a reasonable amount – and a 40-70% ratio is something that can be relied upon, particularly when there are many uncertain factors to be taken into account.

Lack of information, overload of information or doubts about the predictability of an outcome adversely influence one's decision making ability. But if you apply the principles stated in this chapter, you will have enough weapons in your armory to look at your problems differently. Merely by knowing these principle puts you in a better position for making decisions. You won't feel stuck, but rather you will find yourself making some kind of decision and moving forward.

Now let's move on to the next chapter and get the help of AI to solve our decision making problems.

Chapter 6: Use AI and Autopilot Your Decisions

****

"I am not a product of my circumstances. I am a product of my decisions."

— Stephen R. Covey

The modern age is an age of AI (artificial intelligence). We talk about the Internet of Things, big data, robots, and what not- AI is a modern world buzzword.

Science is already exploring human cloning – creating a genetically identical copy of a human with artificial intelligence that can think and behave like a human. That's the level of innovation of technology toward which we are moving.

AI, however, is not something an entirely new concept. The first reference of the term artificial intelligence was made in year 1956 at a conference at Dartmouth College in Hanover, New Hampshire. Although one can argue that a lot has changed, the basic principles of artificial intelligence remain the same.

Let's understand by way of example how a computerized decision-making process works. Let's say you want to apply two simple principles for maintaining the centralized air-conditioning of your house. You want to turn the cooling off when the temperature goes below 74 degree Fahrenheit and keep the air-conditioning to be on only if the temperature goes above 78 from midnight to 6 a.m. You feed in the decision criteria in your computer based on these two needs – between midnight to 6 a.m. the air-conditioning needs to be switched on only if the temperature goes above 78 degree Fahrenheit, or the air-conditioner will be on every time, unless the temperature goes below 74 degrees Fahrenheit.

Therefore, by setting certain formulas, you can create a decision making system for a machine that takes into account the necessary data, applies the principle and recommends a decision based on the principle set for it.

This the simplest example of intelligence created artificially by the human mind through the use of technology. But with technological advancements, many more parameters or criteria of extreme complexities are added to the computer. The concept of the Internet of Things (IOT) is nothing but the expansion of the realm of artificial intelligence, where you connect a network of physical devices, vehicles, home appliances, and other items embedded with electronics, software, sensors, enabling these things to exchange data with each other and make much more complex activities possible through internet connectivity.

A gentleman named Ray Dalio, an American billionaire investor, known to be among the top 100 richest persons alive, runs the private investment banking firm of Bridgewater Associates, one of the world's biggest hedge funds with a portfolio of 160 billion US dollars. If you don't know it, Dalio is a kind of genius, known for integrating a massive amount of historical data about stocks and other financial instruments' trading patterns with computer-driven algorithms to make investment decisions automatically through machines. In effect, Dalio has been able to brilliantly combine *human intelligence* with the *machine intelligence*, thus creating a highly powerful algorithm. These algorithms take massive amounts of historical data, and trends in trading commodities, stocks or other financial instruments; and based on such information, these algorithms make future profitable trading or investment decisions.

Know this Superior AI- Ancient Intelligence

But this is not the only form of AI. Let's talk about another type of AI specific to human beings. Ray Dalio in his bestseller book, *Principles: Life and Work,* terms this as **Ancient Intelligence**, which is much more powerful than *artificial intelligence*. Let's understand how?

In human brains, there is a portion known as the *basal ganglia*. The role of this organ is to put certain behaviours on autopilot that we keep doing on a regular basis. We can harness the potential of this part of our brain to write algorithms to reprogram this other form of AI.

How can we do it?

The Power of Implementation Intentions

It is with the help of ***implementation intentions***. As in the way you can program your air-conditioning system to work by setting the desired algorithm, it's possible for human beings to program themselves through implementation intentions.

Implementation intention is a simple approach of taking action based on the "if-then" approach. It's a self-regulatory strategy in the form of an "if-then" plan that leads to habit formation and behavior modification.

For example, if it's 7 a.m., then it's wake up time. If you have taken bath, then you will sit for silent meditation for 15 minutes. If it is 10 p.m., then it is time to read a great book for 30 minutes before you sleep. Finally, if it's 10.30 p.m., then you need to go to bed.

Above are simple illustrations of implementation intention that indicate that *if one condition happens or is satisfied, then you have to take some specific action.* You set the algorithm for your human machine like this only, and then they follow.

The *if-then* approach triggers your basal ganglia to track your behaviour for a certain period; and soon this puts it on autopilot. It means that things start to happen on an autopilot basis after you have given it some amount of time to settle in.

This approach of setting algorithms based on your ancient intelligence starts with smaller activities, of course. But as you start adding many "if-then" algorithms through the use of this ancient intelligence, your decision making abilities start to enhance. Smaller decisions don't take much time for you – as you have generated a huge subconscious repertoire of many implementation intentions. One you set the simpler implementation intentions, you can start accumulating the algorithms for higher decisions like what's the right way to influence your customers' decisions or what products you need to launch in a new market or what would be the right criteria for diversifying your business operations.

And that's the ultimate AI

Dalio states that traditional AI programming can increase productivity to 100,000 times. Here is how it works. If you make a decision to do the optimal thing once, you save the effort and an enormous amount of willpower of deciding 1,000+ times. You make *100* wise decisions like that and you have just increased your optimizing efficiency 100,000 fold.

Your ancient intelligence can be programmed the way you want, through consistent repetition with the help of implementation intentions. Once you have been reprogrammed based on your "ancient intelligence", you save enough energy to make bigger and more complex decisions, as you start making smaller and routine decisions based on internal pre-set programming.

On the top of this, if someone can explore ways to combine ancient intelligence with artificial machine intelligence, the way Dalio uses in his own trading decisions, then you can make huge number of decisions in a lower number of times. That's the way to explode your growth potential, because ultimately life is all about making decisions – the more you make, the better you become.

Chapter 7: A Proactive Formula for Smart Choices

****

"Nobody's life is ever all balanced. It's a conscious decision to choose your priorities every day." ~ Elisabeth Hasselbeck

How to Make Better Decisions

Let's burst this myth that decision making is some inborn quality or something that is solely gifted to a selected few. Everyone is capable of making better decisions, if the necessary elements of the process are learned and implemented.

There are a few essential elements of decision-making, which if understood well, will empower you to make better and more effective decisions in your life. Once you are aware of these key elements, you will find that you start to make better decisions. Let's understand what they are:

- Effective decision making is focused on *what is important to you.*
- It is *logical and consistent*, because it's based on certain pre-set principles.
- It is *holistic* and takes into account subjective and objective factors related to any problem. It also blends analytical thinking with the intuitive approach.
- It encourages *gathering as much relevant information* as necessary to form an opinion.

Analyse any decision of yours or others, and you will realize that every good decision is comprised of prescribed elements. A good decision is an outcome that is ornamented with all of the above.

But now arises the main question – is there any specific approach to follow that would ensure that the resultant decisions come out as a result of all the above elements.

Precisely then, what are the key criteria of the decision-making process that will ensure that we make best decisions for ourselves and others around us?

The PrOACT Approach

Here is a well-curated decision making approach from **John Hammond, Ralph Keeney and Howard Raiffa,** researchers and authors of the book *Smart Choices* who calls it the PrOACT Model.

Proact is acronym which states the different steps to follow to make better choices.

- **Pr**- Problem
- **O**- Objective
- **A**- Alternative
- **C**- Consequences
- **T** – Trade offs

This approach is, in fact, a proactive method of decision making, as you will understand on your own once you go through this chapter. Let's now dive deeper into the necessary steps:

<u>Problem</u> Identification

The first step is to determine what exactly the problem is.

Let's understand this by way of an example. Assume you wanted to take a coaching class in an academic or professional subject.

How would you identify your problem? You'd start with: which coaching center should you join?

But hang on. Is this the real problem?

If you spend a few moments refining your problem, you'll notice that your problem is how to learn better and not the selection of a coaching center. With the new approach to defining your problem, you widen your thinking perspective and not limit yourself to merely a location.

You've now identified the problem correctly, i.e., how to learn better and more effectively and, accordingly, you'll now start to see the available options.

Maybe you want to consider purchasing an online coaching course that you can pursue in the comfort of your home. Or maybe you sit with few of your friends and ponder the problem and find the solution.

The idea is that you shouldn't immediately jump in and start choosing the right solutions without first really understanding the core of your problem.

In order to make a good choice, you have to state your decision problem very carefully. You have to understand that there are complexities, and you have to avoid unwarranted assumptions and option-limiting prejudices.

Clarify Your Objective

The next step is to clarify your objective.

Once you identify your problem correctly, the next step is identifying the end objective you want to achieve by making a decision.

Let's continue with the previous example of joining a coaching class. Once you started identifying the problem, immediately you began to ponder the end objective you want to achieve by solving it. You realized that your end objective is to learn effectively, at a reasonable cost and with as little inconvenience as possible. Once you clarify your objective, you start seeing the same problem from a different perspective.

Take another example. Assume you have to choose between a morning walk or preparing to participate in a half marathon. Here is how you'll operate. If your objective is to just to maintain a regular and fit body, you would simply choose to go for a quick walk, or jog. But if your objective is to test and stretch your physical limits and run a half marathon or full marathon, then you would decide about adopting the right training regimen and appropriate diet specifications.

The decision between going out for walk for routine exercise versus undergoing professional training for a half marathon depends upon the end objective related to your health.

You have to ask yourself what you want to accomplish most and which of your interests, values, concerns, fears, and inspirations are most relevant for achieving that goal. Thinking through your objective will give direction to your decision making.

Expand Your <u>**Alternatives**</u>

The next step in the PrOACT approach is all about creating alternatives.

You need to be imaginative and creative in determining the alternative solutions for any problem. The first step is to write down all of them or as wide a net as possible of alternatives that come to mind. I know some of these alternatives might not sound that good, when you first list them, but don't fret. We can strike them off later, when we start analysing the various options to reach the best one. Sometimes, the alternative that doesn't sound appealing initially turns out to be your best one. So expand your alternatives – because you don't want to lose out on the best alternative.

Take another example. Assume you want your child to choose a particular field of study or career. You need to check what kind of alternatives you have for him or her based on his skills, interests, strengths, etc.

How good is your child at school, and how good is he or she in sports or extra-curricular activities? Does he or she loves to stay alone or with a few friends, or is he or she more of an extroverted kind of personality? Considering all these factors will help you create many alternatives. Having good alternatives is important for considering all the possible solutions in front of you.

If you didn't have different alternatives, you'd be constantly wondering and worrying whether you had missed out some possibility. You might also regret later not spending little time expanding your alternatives before making the final decision.

Therefore, you should strive for at least a wide range of creative and desirable alternatives because your best decision will come out of your best alternative only.

Understand <u>Consequences</u>

After you have identified multiple alternatives, the next step is to look at the consequences of each.

Assume you are in a corporate job and want to try entrepreneurship. There are different alternatives in front of you. You can do it in the form of a side hustle, like doing something early in the morning before you go to office or in the evening after your work hours. (I wrote my first two books in the evenings while working a full-time day job). Or you may consider jumping full-fledged into the chosen entrepreneurship by quitting your job.

For each of the alternatives, you have to look at the consequences. If you jump out of the job and start your new venture immediately, it might give you instant freedom to do what you want. But, you need to think about your spouse, kids and family responsibilities. You should to be considerate of what stage of life they're in and what kind of financial security they need, while you are investing time building your empire. You know that leaving a job with a monthly fixed income safety zone for a wild ride of entrepreneurship is not an easy decision. So you need to weigh the pros and cons – to analyze if it a good option to put your spouse and family in financial jeopardy, or could you want to do it on the side?

If you are crystal clear about what business you want to start and also have enough savings to run your family and household without compromising their quality of life for the next 2-3 years, of course, after providing for business expenses, then starting a full-time entrepreneurship may not be that risky a proposition. Otherwise, you may think of doing it on the side or until you save enough funds for a rainy day.

You have to look into the consequences of all your options. Accessing the consequences of each will ultimately help you identify those alternatives best suited to meet your end objective.

Consider Trade-offs

The last step in the PrOACT approach is to consider the trade-offs between the various alternatives. You can have different objectives in life and those different objectives might conflict with each other. Look at the previous example. You have the objective of becoming your own boss by starting your own business, but there is another also very important objective of not compromising the quality of life of your family. Sometimes, you have to compromise and take a middle path and sacrifice one or the other.

The trade-off in the above example is to lose sleep by waking up early and working on your side hustle, and also limiting precious family time in the evening to nurture your entrepreneurship dream. But this loss of sleep and the compromise on family time is to ensure eventual financial security and a better life for your family. In most complex decisions, there is no a single, perfect alternative. You have to juggle many balls at the same time. Your job is to choose intelligently among less-than perfect alternatives. For this purpose, you need to address the trade-offs between different alternatives by taking into account your key priorities.

Researchers Hammond, Keeney and Raiffa further suggest that while the above five elements are key in making effective decisions, they go on to discuss three more elements that lead to an overall effective decision-making strategy.

Clarify Your Uncertainties

The future is uncertain and therefore it requires planning for the unforeseen. We cannot plan for everything, but we can plan for the most foreseeable things. For example, you'll want to keep aside certain funds for your son's education, but how much, exactly, depends unknown factors. Will he choose to go for a low cost education like studying the arts or psychology or is he going to choose the costlier medical career. Will he take an education loan to fund his studies or will he ask for funds from you? Will he take a job in the interim? Uncertainties make your choices more difficult. You need to be able to foresee different forms of uncertainties, assessing their likelihood and impact, in order to make effective decisions.

Be Clear about Your Risk Tolerance

You should be clear about your risk tolerance. If you are willing to take some risk of losing some money in short term in order to work on projects that may reward you in future, you will decide differently compared to a person who wants to play it totally safe.

An investor may choose to invest in a low interest-paying bank account to avoid any risk. On other hand, some people choose to place their funds in a highly-rewarding equity stock, but they are mindful of the risks involved.

Quitting a job and starting your own venture poses the risk of failure and maybe you have to go back to 9 to 5, but those who take that risk also stand the chance of getting rewarded with time and financial freedom. The moot point here is – if you know your risk tolerance capacity, the smoother your decision-making process will be. You will choose only those options that match the right level of risk for you.

Consider Linked Decisions

Most decisions are connected to each other. This means whatever you decide today could influence or restrict your choices of tomorrow. Similarly, the objectives or goals you set for your future will influence your choices of today.

If you choose to accept a long-term 5-year exclusive contract that requires you to relocate to a foreign territory, because it offers a considerable increase in your current remuneration, it will immediately impact your other decisions. You would be missing other career opportunities that may come up during that period in your own country. Your decision to stay abroad will also impact your relationships with close friends and extended family members.

Such linked decisions can be effectively made, if you isolate and resolve the near-term issues at first; but you should also assess the impact of all the other issues that may arise due to your main decision.

In the above example, if your key priority is to build your career by investing your time in a new region that pays you well, and you have assessed the impact it will make on other areas of your life, which you believe you can address when they come up, then it helps you to make decisions faster and better.

The above 8 elements approach of the PrOACT Model will divide your decision-making process in simpler steps and highlight the most essential parameters to help you decide better. You just need to brainstorm and come out with the answers to each of elements of the PrOACT model. Once you have introspected and analyzed each of the elements, you can make your decision by focusing on most important criteria for you.By following PrOACT approach, you'll feel a sense of satisfaction because you have already considered all the important criteria and foreseeable aspects for arriving at your decision. This will improve your confidence, you'll strengthen your decision making muscle and make wider and effective decisions.

Let's now move to the next chapter, where you will learn the ways to broaden your thinking perspective and attract better solutions to your decision problems.

Chapter 8: The Solution Is Around You

****

"Very often, when you change your perspective, you see things differently, make different decisions, and get different results."

~Brian Tracy

Not all decisions are equal. Some require extra diligence and care, because the consequence of mistakes can cost us dearly. When we face such decisions, we tend to get anxious: we think we might be missing something, or maybe we are not following the right sequence or steps. We feel that our problem is unique and no one else is able to understand and guide us in the direction of the right solution.

But here is a revelation.

Solution Finders are Givers by Nature

Unless you are planning to launch a rocket to a planet (excluding Mars – SpaceX founder, Elon Musk, has already indicated his plans to set up a human colony there by 2024), there are chances that people have already found the solution to your problem.

There is a common trait in people who have found solutions. Their journey goes like this – first they deeply immerse themselves to find the solution to the problem, in a way that becomes invisible to others. But once they find the solution, they can't help but stop themselves to give the solution back to the world. Budhha left the world in search of his quest to answer why there is suffering in the world and how to end it. But when he became enlightened, he came back to this world only to spread the knowledge.

And this is not specific to any religious or spiritual belief; the concept of giving back appears everywhere. I was listening to an interview with Ray Dalio, the American billionaire, and bestselling author of the book *Principles* (which we already talked about in a previous chapter). He stated that he had had a great amount of success throughout his entire life. He further explained that since he was above 60 years, he doesn't want to focus attention on adding more success to his name; rather, his new life purpose is to create a generation of successful young people. He is ready to provide the necessary guidance and support to the younger generation, so they can succeed.

Do you know why most high-achievers and successful people end up writing a book or getting their biographies done? Because, it's their natural tendency to give back to the world.

Am I sounding a bit preachy?

I heard you say, "yes, kind of."

But my intent is only to show you that most problems of the world already have some solutions. And the best part is the solution-finders want to spread that knowledge, so others willing to explore don't suffer and, instead, gain wisdom from them. Of course, solution-finders won't come knocking at your door, offering you a gift-wrapped solution package. But it works pretty well the other way round – you go out, knock on their door, and chances are you'll find a solution. You must have already heard the saying, "When the student is ready, the teacher will appear."

Don't worry. Most of the time, the solution is around you. Go look out and look for the relevant books, courses, and, if needed, you can seek mentoring from the experts. Of course, there is a cost associated with everything, but sometimes the cost of not deciding or deciding wrongly is greater than investing in solutions.

If you don't decide to invest a little sum, you'll save the money; but it will cost you more time and effort in learning from the trial and error approach. The hard reality is that unsuccessful people are found spending time to save money, whereas successful people will rather spend money to save time. Why is that an important distinction? Because you can always get more money, but you can never get more time.

Gain From Your Competitors

Another strategy for finding solutions is to look at your competitors or the people in the same domain you are working in.

Whenever you are thinking of venturing out for some new product or business, the best course of action is to look at what your competitors are doing. If they are doing well, they must be doing certain things right. Your job is to track them down and see what they are doing right and start implementing those things into your business or decision.

You must have heard the famous quote from Tony Robbins, "Success Leaves Clues". Of course, your competitors won't come and tell you their best strategies (they'd rather keep them as secret); but if you are watchful, you can track their activities and find the subtle cues and thus find the best solution to your problem.

Take a real life example of Sam Walton, the founder of Walmart. In 1954, he took a 12-hour bus ride to see a new kind of checkout line at the Ben Franklin variety stores – which led customers through one central line, rather than to separate counters for kitchen supplies, toiletries, groceries, etc.

He was quite impressed by the solution and immediately implemented it in his own stores. Indeed, throughout his career, Walton kept an eye on what his competitors were doing, even admitting that almost everything he'd ever done had been copied from someone else.

That's why businesses spend so much time, money and effort getting the market intelligence, so that they can save their own resources by applying the tactics already researched and experimented by their competitors to offer better solutions for their consumer problems.

Don't Ignore the Outside View- Use Base Rates

It happens that we often give too much weight to some idea that we personally feel good about and get so obsessed with it that we ignore the outside reality.

I remember a real-life example when I was out in a yet-to-be-fully-developed area in my town. There were not many stores in operation yet, and I found a new restaurant construction work going in full swing. The owner was there and I check the type of restaurant he was planning to start. As anyone would attend a prospective customer, the owner was forthcoming in telling me more about his upcoming business. I asked him what his expectations and growth plans were. Becoming very excited, he cited the example of an upscale restaurant running in some developed area of the town and he was very confident that as a result of his new venture, people would have a similar option available nearby and might just prefer his place.

I was intrigued. Although I didn't want to demoralize him, still I asked him why he thought that way, given that the market in that area was yet to be fully operational. But the young man was energized and stated that the quality and experience he planned to give to his visitors would make his restaurant exceptional.

Later, I made a few more visits to that area, and I didn't see any foodies or party goers flocking around his restaurant. In around three to four months, I noticed that he had shut down.

What was wrong with his decision?

He had ignored the outside view. Had he spent some time analysing outside facts in that area and considered them in his decision making, he would have revisited his decision to open restaurant there. In reality, in that market, around half of the shops that had opened were closed within a six-month period. The footfall of people was very low in that market. Probably, adjacent locals wanted to hang out in places where they could see a vibrant clientele and party-like environment, which was lacking in this area.

That young entrepreneur simply assumed that merely because of the quality of his food and the ambience provided, he would attract and retain customers. He ignored the outside reality. One of the most famous findings in the psychology of prediction is the phenomenon of "*base rate neglect.*"

Base rates means you need to assess the outside view of the goal you are targeting and the probability of achieving it. The real-world occurrence of the instances gives you some probability of what to expect based on that outside view.

Your own instincts and gut feelings are the inside view of the situation from your own perspective. But the actual results of the activities happening in real-life now or in the past is an outside view. The outside view gives you a base rate to guesstimate the probability of how your results could vary.

In the above example, the outside view about opening a restaurant or food joint in a newly-developing locality is not a good idea, because 50% of the new shops had shut down within around six months. There must have been a reason behind this, requiring analysis before making a decision. The young entrepreneur I described above neglected the base rate and simply went ahead in making a huge investment, solely relying on his own judgement and instinct.

However, this doesn't mean that you shouldn't trust your instinct or gut feelings, but at the same time, you should not entirely neglect the outside view or base rates about a particular situation.

How can you use this in a real-life example?

When you approach experts about predicting a future situation, you should ask them base rate questions. This is because they also might be trapped in the inside view when presented with an individual situation; and they, too, might be neglecting base rates.

You should ask them *indicative* rather than *predictive* questions. For example, you should ask your lawyer about the number or percentage of cases like yours that has gotten success in trials – this is the base rate question – and you are asking for *indications* here. You'll get an outside view of the situation by asking such a question.

However, if you simply ask whether your case will succeed in trial, it is an inside view question, and the answer you get might be ignorant of the base rates.

Now once you have taken a base rate view, even from the experts, you should examine your case closely to determine whether it is exactly like others, and therefore, you will meet the same fate – or you now have figured out some unique aspects that make your situation different.

Taking into account the outside view along with your inside view equips you with a holistic understanding of the situation, and, therefore, you can make smarter decisions.

Don't Take Important Decisions When in Stress

As humans, we don't understand other people based merely on physical actions or verbal communication. Rather, we can read faces and expressions and make judgments about what a person is thinking. For example, if your spouse or friend is upset with you, and doesn't speak to you, you understand something is wrong. You also understand non-verbal communication in the form of facial expressions – you can guess the mood of your manager.

But in the case of the disease of "autism," it cripples a person's ability to understand non-verbal communication. The afflicted are blind to non-verbal signals: they only understand explicitly transmitted information and aren't able to read other people's faces.

Why am I telling you all this. Because even non-autistic people can be rendered temporarily autistic in stressful situations and under time pressure. When under stress, we tend to ignore many indirect signals like facial expressions and go into *tunnel vision* mode, devoting our entire attention to the most imminent "threat," meaning the most relevant piece of information. *Tunnel vision* can, for example, sometimes cause police officers to shoot innocent people because they focus so intently on the possible threat of a weapon such that even a black wallet can seem threatening.

If you want to avoid this kind of autistic "seizure," you have to slow down and reduce the stress in your environment. The worse the stress, the more likely you'll become temporarily autistic. And beyond a certain stress level, the logical thought process stops completely and people become very unpredictable.

Try Ooching to Test-Out Any Idea

We are often faced with high-level decisions, where we are unable to predict the results of those decisions. In such situation, most people end up quitting the option altogether, because the stakes are high and results are very unpredictable.

But there is a solution for this. You should use the process of testing the option on a smaller scale, also known as "ooching". In many situations, it's wise to dip your toe in the water rather than dive in headfirst. Deciding upon something based on your *belief* that it will or won't work is a bad strategy compared to trying it on a smaller scale.

Take an example: undergoing an internship is good idea because with minimal time and effort invested, you will know in less time whether you want to pursue that profession or not.

Moreover, we are bad about predicting our future, so instead of doing some guesswork, it is better to test it out – on a smaller level to get a mini-version of what it will look like.

I personally used this "ooching" experiment recently. I was about to XXXnrol in an expensive coaching program, as I thought it would help me expedite my personal growth. But I was not fully convinced of how the outcome would be. Therefore, I used this approach by enrolling in a low-cost mini course with the same instructor. This approach helped me understand his methodology, style, and content; and I was able to test it with a lower investment, and less time and effort before committing fully to the expensive program.

People often get stuck looking at the sheer volume of the activities involved in something and don't get started. They keep delaying taking action until they get the complete picture. But the ooching approach helps you get started at a smaller level, so you can review the mini-outcomes of your activities and enrich your experience in order to take up the further challenges towards your bigger goals.

I hope the methods suggested in this chapter will help you broaden your thinking horizon and prompt you to look around you to find solutions. When you get out of your own head and start looking outside for better alternatives - trying newer things - it significantly enhances your decision-making abilities.

That said, now lets' move to the next section where you'll learn how looking at the future gives you a different perspective to make decisions differently.

Chapter 9: How To Use Future as Your Best Guide?

****

"If you work hard enough and assert yourself, and use your mind and imagination, you can shape the world to your desires."

— Malcolm Gladwell

Decisions of today define the trajectory of one's life and determine how the future will turn out tomorrow.

Life is like a game of golf. When you have taken a position to hit the ball with your club, you need to be extra cautious about the direction in addition to the amount of force you apply. Even if you hit the ball with the right force, a mere two degrees of deviation can land your ball a few hundred meters away from the hole.

The same principles apply to your life decisions as well. Even a minor deviation or error in your decisions can have a major impact, which can take your life in an altogether different direction.

How minor errors can lead to a major disaster in life was proven by an accident that took hundreds of lives. In late 1970s, a New Zealand airline used to fly from New Zealand for sightseeing over Antarctica and would return back in the evening of the same day. On one tragic day in November of 1979, a flight was carrying more than 200 passengers. Accidently, the coordinates of the flight path were pre-set wrong by 2 degrees one night before the next morning flight and, unfortunately, the crew was not informed of it.

The plane started out normally on its way to Antarctica, but instead of being directed in the right direction, it was re-routed in the path of a mountain. By the time the crew members realized the error, it was too late. They couldn't correct the route of the flight and therefore all the passengers died in that accident.

This sad example shows that how future outcomes are dependent on the right decisions we take today. Therefore, doesn't it make sense to put the future scenario in your mind before deciding anything?

Yes, absolutely. In fact, we should think about how the future could be altered by making different types of choices today.

Let's now understand a few resourceful approaches that will prompt you to keep future outcomes in mind first while making any decision.

Follow the 10/10/10 Rule

This rule is pretty straightforward. Before making any big decision in your life, you need to ask yourself how that decision will affect you in the next 10 minutes, the next 10 months, and the next 10 years.

Most of the time, it's our tendency to make decisions based on our short-term emotions. We feel that we need a product or service right now. Have you ever wondered why you make impulse decisions? It's because *your present emotions are very clear and precise, while future emotions are not yet well defined.* Smart salespersons tend to exploit this human tendency to sell more of their products or services. They try to excite us based on that short-term present emotion to influence our decisions. Promotional messages are crafted to trigger instant emotions and unconsciously force you to make an unplanned decision to buy a product – something known as impulse buying (of course, later you regret making that decision).

Here comes the 10/10/10 rule to empower you and equalize the impact of this short- term influence on your emotions. What this rule recommends is whenever you are faced with decision problems, you need to actively think about what your future emotions would be like. You should awaken your future emotions by asking yourself – how would you would feel about your decision in *10 minutes, 10 months,* or *10 years* from the moment of making that decision.

It helps if the future emotions that arise while thinking about the short- and long-term picture sound equally clear, precise, and supportive of your objective. Only then should you decide to go ahead with the alternative.

Take this example. You have two alternatives: either get a subscription for a video gaming application for 3 months or take it for a period of one year. Obviously, to get the benefit of your current emotions, the video gaming company is offering you a one-year subscription at more than 50% off the regular rate. Your current emotions will focus on the huge saving of 50% by going for a one-year subscription.

But if you think from the 10/10/10 perspective and take a future perspective, you will soon realize that taking a one-year plan will make you more addicted to video game playing. Although you are saving money currently, in 10 months or 10 years from the moment of decision, you could be enslaving yourself to an unhealthy habit. With that realization, you can think of an alternate option. Remember the earlier case: "keep $14.99 for other purchases" as an example of decision making in a previous chapter. If you think about alternatives, you can simply replace this habit with a gym membership - a healthier alternative.

Therefore, it boils down to the fact that spending some amount of time checking your emotions by considering the future scenario empowers you to make more beneficial decisions for yourself.

Use Prospective Hindsight

Here is another approach to making decisions keeping the future impact in mind.

Often, we imagine one possible consequence of our actions and base our decisions on that one specific idea of how the future will unfold – this is despite the fact that we have no way of actually predicting the future.

In reality, we can only make a prediction of the future based on the limited aspects we know about. But the future can throw at us many new, unknown, and uncertain things that we probably have not yet experienced in our lives. At this stage, we find ourselves standing at a crossroad -

while we have to make a decision, we have a very limited amount of information we can use to make a prediction of the future outcome.

Although we learned the 40:70 Rule in a previous chapter that addresses making decisions when you have a limited amount of information, there is another approach that will guide you to take the right action in the present moment to avoid a future disaster.

It is a technique called Prospective Hindsight that can help you improve your future vision. The word "prospective" means to imagine a scenario, and the word *hindsight* means to look back from the scenario to the cause of that scenario. It is also known as *project pre-mortem*.

Let's understand how this works. As humans, we are not that good at evaluating future possibilities compared to the actual facts. We can easily post-mortem a fact and find the reasons by constructing an anatomy of the situation. But, unfortunately, we can't do it with the same level of precision in the case of evaluating a future possibility.

Prospective hindsight philosophy helps you to hypothetically go into future and ask yourself a question, *"It's one year from now and the project I started has failed, why?"*, rather than, *"What could be the reasons that lead to future failure?"*

The prospective hindsight approach helps you think broadly about the possible reasons for failure, and once you list those reasons, you'll find yourself better equipped to look at the options that could prevent it.

But prospective hindsight is not merely about thinking about a future disaster scenario. You can imagine a more positive scenario of glorious success. Yu could think of what has led to your success and then improve on those factors. You should use this approach to ensure that you're able to handle any possible success. For example, if you plan to launch a new product, do you have the capability of meeting the demand should it become suddenly successful and popular? Do you have in place the proper infrastructure to produce and distribute your wares, in case the demand explodes? You should also implement a safety factor to stay prepared for unforeseeable circumstances.

Consider the example of the strength of ropes in an elevator: the cables are eleven times stronger than needed for it to function. Engineers calculate how much weight it will transport, what strain will be put on the cables, and which cables will carry that weight – they then multiply the answer by eleven times. Similarly, when engineers construct a bridge, they design it in a way for it to take the load of multiple times the load they sanction, so it can handle any unforeseen circumstances.

We tend to be overconfident in our knowledge and expertise, so it's a good idea to be rather cautious and adjust our predictions based on that fact. The prospective hindsight technique works by using the benefit of a human's ability to analyze actual facts. By imagining future events as actual fact, we are better able to determine the reason for failure or success, helping us to expand our thinking horizon so we can make more informed and better decisions.

The techniques stated in this chapter will help you take the benefit of your future emotions and also the human brain's capabilities to look at the future events as actual facts. All the decisions, we make today are made in order to get better results and feel good in future about those decisions. Therefore the methods stated in this chapter help you see yourself standing in future, as a result of your decisions that you have to take today and this helps you to take decisions more confidently.

Now let's move to the last chapter and we will learn one holistic decision making method.

Chapter 10: 4-Step Process to Make Holistic Decisions

****

"Success emerges from the quality of the decisions we make and the quantity of luck we receive. We can't control luck. But we can control the way we make choices."

— Chip Heath

It's wonderful to see you reaching so far . I welcome you to the last section of this book.

There can't be any better ending except by way of explaining one holistic decision-making method famously known as the WRAP method. Propounded by Chip and Dan Heath, academicians at Stanford University and Duke's University's CASE Center, respectively, this method is not some short-cut quick-fix kind of formula;

rather it is a holistic approach to make better decisions.

Most people do not tend to make decisions systematically; rather they do it in a haphazard manner. There could be many reasons for this random kind of approach.

People often realize that they are short of time and need to make fast decisions. At times, although they have limited knowledge or understanding, they presume they have all the information or have an I-figured-it-all-out over-confidence that prompts them to decide hastily.

Sometimes, people are just lazy and don't want to put even minimal effort in finding the relevant information for making effective decisions. In some cases, they don't know how to get more information by asking the right set of questions; and, therefore, they end up compromising with low-quality decision making.

Thus, most of the reasons for hasty, low-quality decisions generally can be put into only a few categories, like a shortage of time, lack of information, over-confidence, and lack of clarity on the right set of information required, etc.

The W.R.A.P. approach addresses all the important aspects related to effective decision making. The focus of the approach is to enable better decision making by focusing on often-ignored or overlooked factors that might have a bigger ramification in the long run in our lives.

W.R.A.P is acronym, as explained below, where each letter signifies a step-by-step approach to arrive at the best decision for any set of problems.

W- Widen your alternatives

R- Reality-test your assumptions

Attain Distance before making decisions

P- Prepare to be wrong

Let's expound upon each of these factors one by one.

<u>Widen</u> Your Alternatives:

We talked in one of the previous chapters about the fact that people tend to make decisions only in yes or no answers when asked some question. Assuming you are a health-conscious person, trying to stop eating junk fund. Suppose a friend asks you if you wish to order pizza. If you simply think of the answer in only yes or no, you are not going to be happy with any of your decisions. If you say yes, you'll be feeling guilty about eating junk food, while if you say no, then you'll feel sad about killing your desires.

You know already by now that you don't have to limit yourself to yes or no. Rather, you should go one level higher and start exploring your options. You should ask, what could other options be from which you can choose? Maybe you can simply order a fresh salad from Subway - adjacent to the pizza shop - or go for healthy vegetable soup.

Widening your alternatives requires you to do some imaginative and creative thinking. You need to be open to explore possibilities. Whether you're choosing food from a restaurant menu or are finalizing a destination for your next vacation, you need to explore the best possible alternatives. Whether you are applying for new jobs and looking for the best companies to work for or are launching a new product or service in the market, you should first think broadly about all the possibilities. Because you never know: a least probable option (at the stage of exploration) might turn out to be the best possible solution, once you research and analyze the possible outcomes considering the given circumstances and other relevant factors.

There is one wonderful approach for widening your options known as the **laddering approach**. Laddering is a staggered approach of broadening your exploration of alternatives. It suggests that whenever you need to make a decision about something, you should start by looking *locally* in and around your own area. For example, if you want to open a restaurant in a particular locality, you need to first start looking at current restaurants and what cuisine will have more demand. You then check out the numbers and types of Chinese, continental, Italian, or other cuisine restaurants. By looking at a variety of options, you broaden your understanding of the different available options in the market.

The next step in the laddering approach is to go beyond the local and think **regionally**. Now you need to look around the whole area to see the restaurants that are running well. By thinking at the next region level, you'll get more options to help you decide better.

But you don't need to stop at the regional level. You can move ahead and explore the far distance, maybe look at what's happening **internationally**. This will broaden your thinking horizon about what's working well in other countries and how you can gain the first mover advantage by looking at the early trends.

I recalled an approach suggested by Tony Robbins named, *"**broadening the reference fabric**"*- meaning you need to enhance your understanding of the subject by exposing your mind to different types of reference points. With the enhanced reference fabric, your thinking horizon broadens and you become more creative to generate better ideas. After all, most creativity is nothing but a fusion of different ideas taken from all kinds of places or people and coming out with your own unique idea.

Take the example of Scott Adams, the famous cartoonist of the Dilbert series. He had an idea in his head to explore things in a funny way, but he didn't consider himself to be as good as a stand-up comedian. While he soon realized that he has artistic abilities, he didn't see himself as an artist like Picasso. He loved to talk about meaningless situations in the corporate environment.

By exploring various options, Adams broadened his reference fabric, and then the magical "*idea-fusion*" happened. He came out with a funny, artistic cartoon series focusing on the office environment and its meaningless discussions. The Dilbert cartoon series was born, an altogether unique project that no one had done in the past. That's how widening your alternatives works to improve your creativity and present you with different alternatives.

Remember your best decisions will always come from one of your best alternatives. So, don't act hastily and ignore your best possible alternatives.

Reality-test your Assumptions

People almost behave in an autopilot mode. They have their own assumptions about things, and they get influenced by these assumptions, so they end up making low-quality and ineffective decisions.

As you have already learned, we unconsciously act under the influence of confirmation bias, which means we always try to find evidence that proves our beliefs to be true. It so happens that when someone is presenting a new or different idea, we tend to reject any new idea outright that doesn't match with our existing beliefs.

We tend to justify our reasons by giving one or another argument like, "This product or service won't work in my city or town", or "I've not seen any such thing in my whole experience, so it's not a good idea to explore", or other such arguments. You try to assign as many reasons as you can to confirm your bias towards a particular view. Warren Buffet puts it very aptly: *"What the human being is best at doing is interpreting all new information so that their prior conclusions remain intact."*

Precisely, our assumptions about various things, people, and events are strongly influenced by confirmation bias. This requires sincere work to counter those self-imposed limitations in our thinking. Here are a few approaches that would be helpful to reality test your assumption about any alternatives, before you make a conclusion and any decision.

    a. *Use Critical Thinking:* You can start by asking a discomforting question - a question against your preconceived notions or pre-set beliefs. If you decide based on an old assumption that things will continue to work in a particular way, you need to ask tough questions like, "Is there a possibility that you will get laid off or fired from the job you consider a safe haven and what would be the reasons? or "what if the market dynamics catapult and you end up sitting with obsolete products or unwanted service offerings?"

This approach is also known as black hat thinking, one of the six thinking approaches suggested by Edward De Bono in his best seller book, *Six Thinking Hats*. The approach requires you to critically examine everything that can go wrong about your decisions and then carefully assess the different alternative based on your most important parameters. Critical thinking prepares you to handle the worst case scenarios and triggers your imagination to foresee and examine various alternatives.

b. *Zoom Out-* This approach requires closely looking at the finer details of the situation by getting into the nuts and bolts of each alternative. You need to closely examine the various aspects or activities involved in your preferred alternative and the level of knowledge or skill sets required to handle them. This approach intends to rule out any alternative, where due to a missing link or some key technical requirement, a higher cost, or any other requirement, you might end up losing financially and emotionally.

c. *Take baby steps*- Use the ooching approach you have learned already and get your feet wet before you jump fully into the water. Why just rely on your prediction when you can see the results of your preferred alternative in a smaller version. Ooching takes the guesswork out of the job and helps you directly experience the pros and cons of your best alternative.

d. You can do a reality test of your assumption by taking the outside view or base rate, as already discussed. This requires you to examine the situation from the outside by taking a holistic and bigger picture view. Whatever alternative you're thinking of, you can do research on the outcome of the decisions taken by people in similar situations. Remember the example of opening a restaurant in a high-street traffic area; you need to check the actual success rate of the restaurants opened in that area and take it into consideration before you make decisions.

Attain Distance:

Can you see your own glasses when you have them on?

No, because you see through them. Only a person from the outside can tell you how your glasses look (unless you remove them and see on your own).

Yes, you cannot see something objectively when you are closely associated with it. It is the same when we are too closely attached with your ideas. You love your ideas like your own babies – and, therefore, they always sound like the best ones. Who sees fault in their own babies?

We remain stuck in the status quo, because we don't step back to see things from a distance. But when reviewing an alternative, it is of the utmost necessity to somehow create a distance from your own thinking.

How do you create a distance? It's by shifting your perspective.

You can look at your problem as some of a friend's problem, and not yours. This immediately helps you to see it outside of your head. Now you need to analyze what would you advise your friend to do in a similar situation.

Often, we are clouded by our own circumstances and prejudices while making decisions for ourselves. But when we need to advise our friends, we tend to become more objective. You might remember the example from a previous chapter, where you chose to advise your friend to go to his or her boss to clarify a situation (you took an independent view here), but if you were to take similar action in a situation applicable to you, you will find yourself influenced by the emotions of fear, anxiety or "what-will-he-say-or-think?" kind of thoughts. Bestselling Author and Speaker John. C. Maxwell has put this rightly in his below words:

> *"One of the reasons that problem solving is so difficult is that we are often too close to the problems to truly understand them."*

Shifting your perspective about alternatives provides you with an altogether different and maybe better alternative. Let me tell you a story showing the huge benefit of shifting one's perspective in problem solving.

Mike Abrashoff was the captain of a ship named, the USS Benefold, which became one of the best ships in the United States Navy in his captaincy. The staff under his leadership were committed to challenge the *status quo* in every area. I'll share one specific example where looking at a situation by attaining distance provides a major shift in perspective and saves time, effort, and lots of money.

Here was the brilliant idea. The ship was required to be painted every month, necessitating around one month's time to cover the entire ship. This painting was necessary because rust stains mar the finish and run down the sides. One sailor suggested to Abrashoff that swapping the ferrous metal fasteners (nuts, bolts, etc.) topside with stainless steel (which doesn't rust in salt water) would eliminate a lot of repetitive work. It was a no-brainer, but no one earlier had ever thought it from a different perspective. Abrashoff adopted the idea and the ship not only went ten months between paintings, but the entire Navy adopted the program. Every ship now uses a stainless steel topside – saving millions of dollars – all because there was a shift in perspective in looking at familiar things.

Prepare to be Wrong

The last string of the WRAP approach is about being prepared to be wrong. We are often over-confident, thinking our decisions will turn out to be right, but the hard reality is that we don't' know what is there in future and how it will unfold.

This approach of always thinking that our decisions will turn out the way we want inhibits are desire to explore the negative aspects of the decision-making process.

There is a different approach that requires us to be prepared for bad outcomes called ***premortem***. Premortem is a managerial strategy in which a project team imagines that a project has failed and then works backwards to see what potentially could lead to the failure of other projects.

An 2007 article[6] from the Harvard Business Review states that unlike a typical critiquing session, in which project team members are asked what *might* go wrong, the premortem approach operates on the assumption that the "patient" has died, and so asks what *did* go wrong.

This is an imagination of a worst case scenario and then thinking backwards about the reasons for the failure and what you could have done to address the reasons that led to it.

Moreover, if you are prepared to be wrong in any situation, it allows you to make alternative plans to which you can transition.

Let's take our earlier example of opening a Chinese restaurant in a high-street traffic area. Start by apply the premortem approach. Assume that restaurant has flopped and try to find the reasons for the failure. You might come out with reasons like:

---

[6] https://hbr.org/2007/09/performing-a-project-premortem

- You couldn't get hold of the right chefs to offer a delicious cuisine.
- Probably your pricing was not appropriate for the area.
- Maybe you didn't market or position your restaurant well in the eyes of your perspective customer.
- Maybe the location of the restaurant was too much on a corner, so it attracted only a few customers.
- Maybe you didn't offer many alternatives.
- Probably, you just added to the competition already there.

This approach can provide you with many reasons that hypothetically could be leading to your failure. The approach therefore equips you to work cautiously on everything that could bring a bad outcome.

If things don't go the way you thought despite being cautious about the pitfalls, preparing to be wrong helps you to devise backup plans. You would prepare

Plan B or Plan C if your key Plan A doesn't succeed. This will help you transition smoothly to different plans. You can think of changing the cuisine or your restaurant to multi-cuisine. Maybe you can now think of attracting corporate clients by putting a good marketing plan in place.

All in all, if you are prepared in advance to be wrong, you'll be able to control the situation more easily than a situation where you haven't taken into account the untoward scenario.

To sum up, the WRAP Formula empowers you with vast number of alternatives to choose from. It warns you to do a realty test of the situation with wide open eyes, shift your perspective to see the alternatives objectively, and finally be fully prepared if things don't go the way you thought.

Therefore WRAP formula helps you take a holistic view of any situation and make a decision that will show the full utilization of your cognitive abilities and instincts. This approach helps you deconstruct complex problems holistically into well-examined alternatives and thus enables you to make smarter decisions in every situation.

Final Thoughts

****

"Nothing happens until you decide. Make a decision and watch your life move forward."

Oprah Winfrey

Congratulations! You made it to the end in this running-like-mad world where people often quit every another project they start.

I sincerely believe that you must have gotten a few wisdom nuggets out of this book, so that you can start implementing them in your life.

In fact, you don't have to wait for some big project to start applying the techniques learned in this book. You are making decisions every moment of your life, so you can start with any of the choices you want to make right now and begin applying the principles.

Peter Drucker, a famous management consultant, once rightly stated:

> **"Making good decisions is a crucial skill at every level."**

Decision making is and will always remain a highly-in-demand cognitive skill. Like any other skill, you can develop it with consistent practice. You need to keep your own false and limiting presumptions aside and expand your thinking horizon. You can start by questioning your existing cognitive biases by applying critical thinking and using your creativity and imagination to expand the number of alternatives in area of your decision.

Don't let the fear of failure hinder you from taking action. Remember this quote from Maimonides, a Jewish philosopher who said, ***"The risk of a wrong decision is preferable to the terror of indecision."***

At the end, I urge you to start using these principles in your day-to-day lives. Keep refreshing these principles by consistently implementing them in your small and big decisions, and sooner or later, you'll find yourself making your decisions more confidently and taking 100% charge of your life.

I wish you nothing but grand success in your life.

Cheers

Som Bathla

Your Free Gift:

Did you download your Free Gift already?

Click Below and Download your **Free Report**

Learn 5 Mental Shifts To Turbo-Charge Your Performance In Every Area Of Your Life - in Next 30 Days!

You can also grab your FREE GIFT Report through this below URL:

http://sombathla.com/mentalshifts

DISCLAIMER

be taken as expert instruction or commands. The reader is responsible for his or her own actions.

The author makes no representations or warranties with respect to the accuracy or completeness of the contents of this work and specifically disclaims all warranties, including without limitation warranties of fitness for a particular purpose. No warranty may be created or extended by sales or promotional materials. The advice and recipes contained herein may not be suitable for everyone. This work is sold with the understanding that the author is not engaged in rendering medical, legal or other professional advice or services. If professional assistance is required, the services of a competent professional person should be sought. The author shall not be liable for damages arising here from. The fact that an individual, organization of website is referred to in this work as a citation and/or potential source of further information does not mean that the author endorses the information the individual, organization to website may provide or recommendations they/it may make. Further, readers should be aware that Internet websites listed in this work might have changed or disappeared between when this work was written and when it is read.

Adherence to all applicable laws and regulations, including international, federal, state, and local governing professional licensing, business practices, advertising, and all other aspects of doing business in any jurisdiction in the world is the sole responsibility of the purchaser or reader.

Made in the USA
Columbia, SC
27 November 2018